MOCK CONGRESS WORKBOOK

Simulating the House of Representatives

SECOND EDITION

By

Sara Parker
Chabot College

and

Katie Zuber
Vassar College

❁ cognella® | ACADEMIC PUBLISHING

Bassim Hamadeh, CEO and Publisher
Kassie Graves, Director of Acquisitions and Sales
Jamie Giganti, Senior Managing Editor
Carrie Montoya, Manager, Revisions and Author Care
Miguel Macias, Senior Graphic Designer
Kaela Martin, Associate Editor
Natalie Lakosil, Licensing Manager
Alia Bales, Associate Production Editor

Printed in the United States of America

cognella
academic publishing
www.cognella.com   800-200-3908

Contents

Introductory Letter, Disclosure   1

Full List of Participants   3

Diagrams of Classroom Set-Up   9

Schedule of Simulation   11

Representative Instructions   15

Leadership Instructions   17

Lobbyist Instructions   21

Witness Instructions   25

Quick Reference Bills   31

Bill 1: H.R.1526 Drone Aircraft Privacy
and Transparancy Act of 2017   33

Bill 2: H.R. 2479 Leading Infrastructure
for Tomorrow's America Act   37

Bill 3: H.R. 610 Choices in Education Act of 2017   41

Bill 4: H.R. 15 Raise the Wage Act   45

Bill 5: H.R. 2272 Clean Ocean
and Safe Tourism Anti-Drilling Act   49

Bill 6: H.R. 2695 Environmental Justice Small
Grants Program Act of 2017   51

Bill 7: H.R. 83 Mobilizing Against Sanctuary Cities Act   55

Bill 8: H.R. 2437 Back the Blue Act of 2017   57

Committee of the Whole Debating Rules   59

Appendix   63

        Representative Worksheet   65

        Leader Worksheet   71

        Lobbyist Worksheet   75

        Witness Worksheet   79

        Rules Sheet   85

Introductory
Letter

Dear Student,

Mock Congress is an in-class exercise meant to simulate the legislative branch of government. It is based on the organization and processes of the House of Representatives. The people, bills, procedures, and details of the House of Representatives are as realistic as possible. Of course, this is an exercise for the classroom, so modifications were necessary. Despite the necessity of such modifications, we have attempted to keep the realities of lawmaking in Congress present and legitimate.

Like any simulation, this exercise will only give you a sampling of the real process. The more effort you put in, the better you prepare, and the more seriously you take your assigned role, the more valuable and fun the experience will be for everyone.

There are four different roles that you might have: a *representative*, a *leader* (a representative with additional responsibilities), a *witness*, or a *lobbyist*. This workbook includes all of the information you need to understand your role and how the simulation will work. In addition, there are many other resources available for you to learn about Congress. Depending on your role, knowing more than your peers will allow you to control the debate, reduce the likelihood that you will be swayed by lobbyists, better convince your peers of your position, broker deals between parties and congressional factions, or simply to come across as believable and trustworthy (something that should not be underestimated). Therefore, we encourage you to go above and beyond the resources provided here and to use this simulation as an opportunity to learn more about how Congress works!

Sincerely,
Sara Parker, PhD
Political Science
Chabot College

Katie Zuber, PhD
Political Science
Vassar College

Disclosure

This workbook is meant to be, first and foremost, a learning experience, not an exact reenactment of Congress or the House of Representatives.

- Not all legislation used for the purposes of this exercise is presented in its entirety. Sections of bills have been eliminated in order to keep the length of the exercise manageable. When legislation has been edited, it is so noted. The full text of all legislation is public information and can be accessed through the Library of Congress at: <http://thomas.loc.gov/home/thomas.php>.
- The experts who give testimony before the committees simulated in this exercise are not based on real life. Although some of the titles or positions of the witnesses in this workbook are real, their roles as witnesses regarding the legislation featured here is purely fictional.
- The lobbyists that are utilized for the purposes of this exercise are not based on the actual work of those organizations identified. Although the organizations may be real, their role in lobbying for or against the bills used in this exercise is purely fictional.
- The representatives utilized for the purposes of this exercise were chosen in order to reflect the diversity of Congress. Real representatives are used so that students may rely on up-to-date, accessible information that will enable them to connect with their government. Students should research the positions of representatives and make their best effort to remain true to their public positions on legislative issues.

Full List of Participants

List of Mock Congress Participants and Committee Assignments

Representatives are based on the 116th Congress (2019–2021)

REPRESENTATIVES

*The parentheses after the name of the representative tell you two things: whether the representative is a Democrat (D) or a Republican (R), and what state they are from.

LEADERSHIP

1. Speaker of the House Nancy Pelosi (D-CA)
    http://pelosi.house.gov/
    http://www.speaker.gov/

2. Majority Leader Steny Hoyer (D-MD)
    http://hoyer.house.gov/
    http://www.majorityleader.gov/

3. Majority Whip Jim Clyburn (D-SC)
    https://clyburn.house.gov/
    http://www.majoritywhip.house.gov/

4. Minority Leader Kevin McCarthy (R-CA)
    http://kevinmccarthy.house.gov/
    http://www.republicanleader.gov/

5. Minority Whip Steve Scalise (R-LA)
   https://scalise.house.gov/about
   https://www.republicanwhip.gov/

Transportation and Infrastructure Committee

6. CHAIR: Peter A. DeFazio (D-OR)

   http://defazio.house.gov/

7. Antonio Delgado (D NY)
   https://delgado.house.gov/

8. John Garamendi (D-CA)
   http://garamendi.house.gov//

9. Dina Titus (D-NV)
   http://titus.house.gov/

10. Lizzie Fletcher (D-TX)
    https://fletcher.house.gov/

11. Jesús García (D-IL)
    https://chuygarcia.house.gov/

12. Abby Finkenauer (D-IA)
    https://finkenauer.house.gov/

13. Sam Graves (R-MO)
    https://graves.house.gov/

14. John Katcko (R-NY)
    http://katko.house.gov/

15. Carol Miller (R-WV)
    https://miller.house.gov/

16. Mark Meadows (R-NC)
    http://meadows.house.gov/

17. Scott Perry (R-PA)

http://perry.house.gov/

Natural Resources Committee Representatives

18. CHAIR: Raúl Grijalva (D-AZ)

http://grijalva.house.gov/

19. Joe Neguse (D-CO)

https://neguse.house.gov/

20. Debbie Dingell (D-MI)

https://debbiedingell.house.gov/

21. Darren Soto (D-FL)

http://soto.house.gov/

22. Paul Tonko (D-NY)

https://tonko.house.gov/

23. Rob Bishop (R-UT)

http://robbishop.house.gov/

24. Don Young (R-AK)

http://donyoung.house.gov/

25. Paul Gosar (R-AZ)

http://gosar.house.gov/

26. Liz Cheney (R-WY)

http://cheney.house.gov/

Education and Labor Committee Representatives

27. CHAIR: Robert C. "Bobby" Scott (D-VA)

http://bobbyscott.house.gov/

28. Suzanne Bonamici (D-OR)

http://bonamici.house.gov/

29. Joe Courtney (D-CT)
    https://courtney.house.gov/

30. Marcia L. Fudge (D-OH)
    https://fudge.house.gov/

31. Lucy McBath (D-GA)
    https://mcbath.house.gov/

32. Virginia Foxx (R-NC)
    http://foxx.house.gov/

33. Glen Grothman (R-WI)
    http://grothman.house.gov/

34. Tim Walberg (R-MI)
    https://walberg.house.gov/

Judiciary Commitee Representatives

35. CHAIR: Jerrold Nadler (D-NY)

    https://nadler.house.gov/

36. Hakeem Jeffries (D-NY)
    http://jeffries.house.gov/

37. Sheila Jackson Lee (D-TX)
    https//jacksonlee.house.gov/

38. Karen Bass (D-CA)
    https://bass.house.gov/

39. Jamie Raskin (D-MD)
    https://raskin.house.gov/

40. Doug Collins (R-GA)
    https://dougcollins.house.gov/

41. Martha Roby (R-AL)
    http://roby.house.gov/

42. Kelly Armstrong (R-ND)
   https://armstrong.house.gov/

EXPERTS

43. Witness A: (1) Senior Education Policy Specialist with the National Conference of State Legislatures; (2) Director of the U.S. Fish and Wildlife Agency
   (Post-Witness role: Jim Banks (R-IN) https://banks.house.gov/, *Education and Labor Committee)*

44. Witness B: (1) oil and gas well drilling expert; (2) Co-Chair of the National Coalition for Public Education
   Post-Witness role: Jahana Hayes (D-CT) https://hayes.house.gov/, *Education and Labor Committee*

45. Witness C: (1) Executive Director of the Electronic Privacy Information Center; (2) Executive Director of the United States Conference of Mayors
   (Post-Witness role: Thomas Massie (R-KY) http://massie.house.gov/, *Transportation and Infrastructure Committee)*

46. Witness D: (1) Acting Director of U.S. Immigration and Customs Enforcement; (2) Research Fellow at the Brookings Institute's Center for Technology Innovation
   (Voting as: André Carson (D-IN) https://carson.house.gov/, *Transportation and Infrastructure Committee)*

LOBBYISTS

47. American Civil Liberties Union for part 1 & 2 of simulation
   (Voting as: Grace Napolitano (D-CA) https://napolitano.house.gov *Natural Resources Committee)*

48. Chamber of Commerce for part 1 & 2 of simulation
   (Voting as: Doug Lamborn (R-CO) https://lamborn.house.gov/, *Natural Resources Committee)*

49. Sierra Club for part 1 & 2 of simulation
   (Voting as: Mike Johnson (R-LA) http://mikejohnson.house.gov/, *Judiciary Committee)*

50. National Education Association for part 1 & 2 of simulation
   (Voting as: Pramila Jayapal (D-WA) http://jayapal.house.gov/, *Judiciary Committee)*

Diagrams of Classroom Set-Up

Classroom set-up for Committee Work

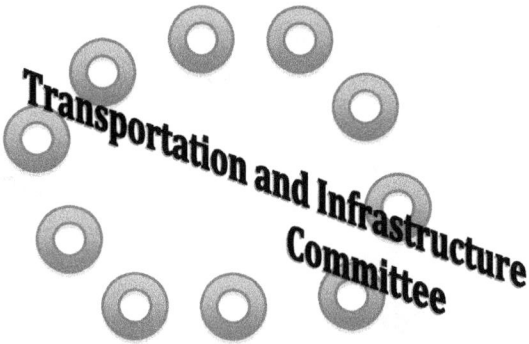

Transportation and Infrastructure Committee

Education and Labor Committee

Students sit in circle in their committees. Make sure to reserve one chair for the witness where everyone will be able to hear and ask questions.

Signs on wall will identify committees.

Natural Resources Committee

Judiciary Committee

Allow as much space as possible between the groups for people to mingle with one another.

Door – depending on your classroom situation, you may be able to hold private meetings in the hallway, outside, or in a nearby space.

Table that witnesses, lobbyists, and/or leadership may use. This is also where students will find their nametag, which should be put on prior to joining their committee, giving testimony, or lobbying.

Diagram of Classroom set-up for Floor Debate

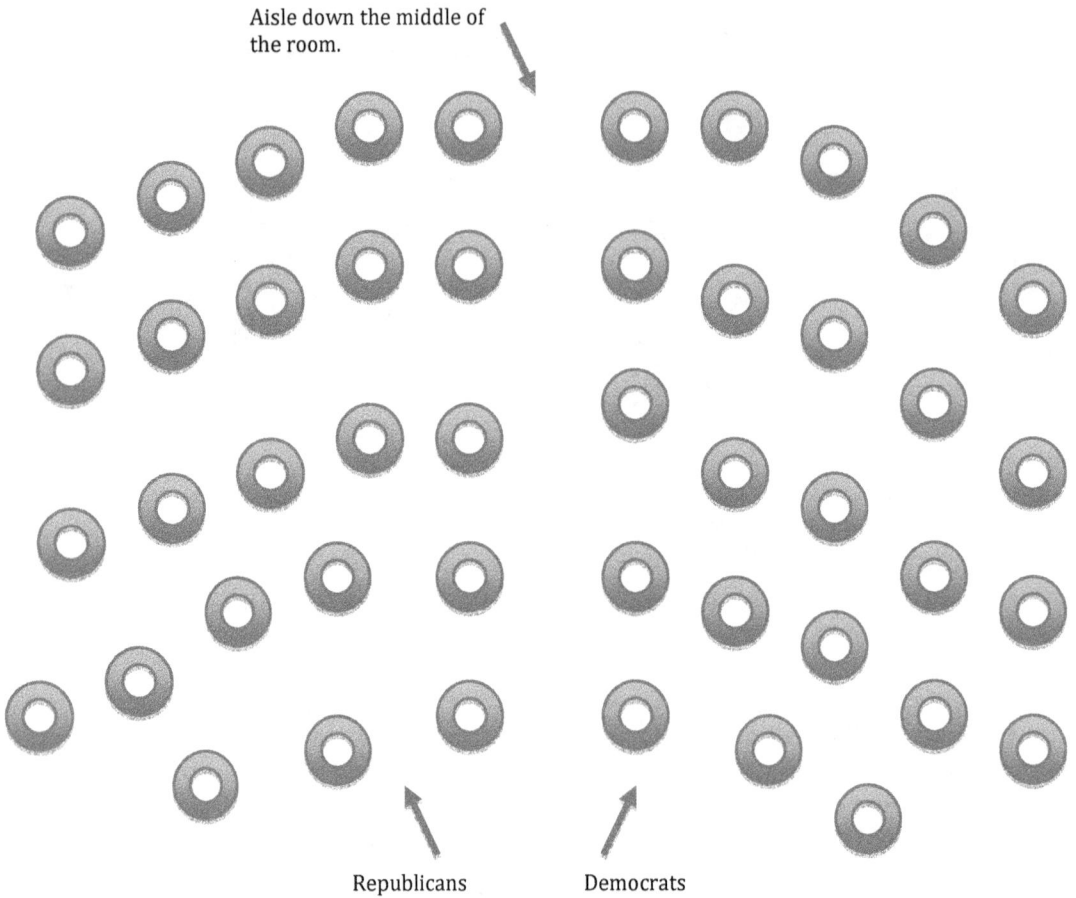

Aisle down the middle of the room.

Republicans   Democrats

Speaker of the House stands at a podium at the front of the room.

Door. Instructor will meet briefly with the Speaker at the start of class. Representatives may mingle, talk strategy with their leadership and/or rehearse their remarks.

Instructor sits at a table at the front of the room to keep time.

Schedule of Simulation

Mock Congress Schedule

There are three parts to the simulation: I) online preparation; II) committee work; III) floor debate. Your instructor will go over the simulation, assign roles, and explain how the three parts of the simulation will be incorporated into your course schedule. Read the instructions for your role in advance of starting the simulation.

Part I. Online Preparation—Students learn about their roles. (Witnesses and lobbyists have two roles, but must only learn about their primary roles.)
Activity:

1. Complete the worksheet for your assigned role.
2. Learn the roles of other students in your class.
3. Identify who the leaders are.

Assignment: Study the bills your committee will work on.

Part II. Committee Work—Witness hearings; bills are debated and modified.
Activity:

1. Representatives sit in committee and introduce themselves to others. Leaders and lobbyists are free to move as they wish.
2. The chair of each committee will call the meeting to order and facilitate introductions. Each representative should state their name, where they are from, and their initial thoughts on each bill.

3. The first of two **witnesses will arrive at each committee. Conversations should cease, and you should arrange the chairs so that everyone can see and hear the witness.**

4. The **witness will introduce him- or herself, make brief opening remarks, and take questions from the committee. The chair of the committee should facilitate the questioning, which should last approximately 10 minutes per witness.**

5. Repeat steps 3 and 4 with the second witness. After each hearing, thank the witness. **After both witnesses testify, move on to discussion of the bills.** *Witnesses adopt secondary roles to become representatives upon completion of their testimony. They will join their assigned committee as representatives at that time.*

6. For each bill, **decide whether to "kill" it, alter it (known as "marking it up"), or pass it as is. You may want to take votes periodically to see where the committee is on each bill. Do not kill a bill lightly. Make every effort first to accommodate diverse opinions, trade favors, and craft compromises.**

7. The chair (or a designee) is responsible for keeping **careful notes on any modifications to the bills.**

8. While all representatives should be focused on committee work, **it is OK to have side conversations with other legislators, to visit other committees, to speak with lobbyists, or House leaders. Do be aware, however, that things may happen in committee that you will miss if you do so.**

9. Your instructor will announce when it is time to wrap up committee work (this will require finalizing any modifications to the bills and taking **final votes).**

10. If one or both of the bills passes out of committee, rip out a rules sheet recommendation (in this workbook), and turn it in to your instructor. This is merely a *recommendation. Final decisions on the rules to accompany each bill will be determined by the* **rules committee (the instructor or designee).**

11. The instructor will either **announce the final list of bills to pass out of committee (and make note of any modifications to those bills) or announce how this information will be made available to the class prior to floor debate.**

12. The Speaker of the House, in consultation with the majority party leadership, must **schedule legislation on the calendar (determine the order that bills will be considered on the floor).** *Lobbyists adopt secondary roles to become representatives upon completion of committee work. They will participate in the floor debate along with everyone else.*

Assignment: Prepare arguments for or against each of the bills to pass out of committee and make a preliminary assessment on how you plan to vote.

Part III. Floor debate—Legislation is debated and voted on.

Activity:

1. Representatives are encouraged to mingle until the Speaker **calls the House to order. Republicans sit on one side of the aisle and Democrats on the other.**
2. The Speaker will introduce bills on the agenda one at a time along with the rules that pertain to that bill (as determined by the rules committee).
3. If and when **amendments are proposed (only if allowed by the rules that govern that bill), debate will switch from the bill to the amendment. The Speaker will allocate a set time to debate the amendment. When debate on the amendment is over, a vote on the amendment will take place. If the amendment passes, debate resumes over the now amended bill. If the amendment fails, debate resumes over the original bill. Please refer to the floor debate information (in this workbook) for more detailed instructions about floor debate procedures.**
4. When time for debate on each bill is up, the Speaker will call for a final vote. The instructor or a designee is the official timekeeper and vote counter.
5. To vote: All those in favor say "Yea" (raise hands), all those opposed say "Nay" (raise hands). Voting will be conducted by a show of hands. Hands that are not clearly identifiable as "raised" will be excluded from the vote.
6. Once the vote is in, the instructor or a designee will record the passage or failure of the bill, and the Speaker will introduce the following bill along with its accompanying rules.
7. The simulation ends when all bills on the calendar have been voted on or at the instructor's discretion.

Representative Instructions

About Your Role

Whether you are a Democrat or Republican, from a rural district or an urban one, part of the current majority or the minority, it is important to remember that representatives are elected by the members of their district to be their voice in the House of Representatives.

You are responsible for working with other representatives (mostly in committee) to craft legislation. In committee, you will work to pass, kill, or modify bills as you see fit. Upon learning what bills have passed out of committee and will be debated on the floor, you will prepare arguments for or against each bill. Your goal is to perform these tasks in such a way as to protect the interests of the people who elected you—your constituents.

This task is not always easy, and there will be many competing pressures. You need to think about your own philosophy regarding representation. Do you see yourself as a *trustee,* whom John F. Kennedy describes as follows?

> The voters selected us, in short, because they had confidence in our judgment and our ability to exercise that judgment from a position where we could determine what were their own best interests, as a part of the nation's interests. This may mean that we must on occasion lead, inform, correct and sometimes even ignore constituent opinion, if we are to exercise fully that judgment for which we are elected.[1]

Or do you see yourself as a *delegate,* as described here?

---

[1] Excerpt from *Profiles in Courage* by John F. Kennedy.

It cannot be pretended that a representative is to be the organ of his will alone; for then, he would be so far despotic. He must be the organ of others—of whom? Not of the nation, for the nation deputes him not; but of his constituents, who alone know, alone have trusted, and can alone displace him. And if it be his province and his duty, in general, to express the will of his constituents, to the best of his knowledge, without being particularly informed thereof, it seems impossible to contend that he is not bound to do so when he is so especially informed and instructed.[2]

To what degree are you willing to prioritize national interests over local interests? Short-term gains over long-time ones? To what degree are you willing to compromise in exchange for progress, versus holding fast to either your campaign promises, personal beliefs, or perceived constituent demands? To what degree do you see these as incompatible goals?

Relationships with other representatives (from your own party and others) and relationships with lobbyists will inform your approach to the legislative process. You must consider the degree to which you are willing or interested in fostering these relationships.

ADVICE

- Remain in character during the simulation. Even if the beliefs of the representative you have been assigned differ from your own, challenge yourself to play the role. This will afford you the opportunity to see things from an alternative perspective.
- Be creative! The more fun you have, the more fun it is for everyone. Prepare, bring in information, and contribute something unique to the simulation.
- Utilize the witnesses: The expert testimony provided at the hearing is your opportunity to ask questions that will help you make a more educated decision on behalf of your constituents.
- You may not be able to get a compromise if you approach a single bill or a single aspect of a bill at a time.
- Rely on your leaders for advice and guidance, but do be an independent thinker.
- Remember to think about what perspective someone else is speaking from—lobbyists, other representatives, leadership, etc. What are their goals? How do they differ from yours? Is there any overlap?
- While your primary focus should be the bills in your own committee, your ability to stay up to date on the progress of bills in other committees will be to your advantage.
- Be respectful.

---

[2] Commonwealth of Virginia, General Assembly, *Journal of the Senate*, 1812.

Leadership Instructions

About Your Role

Whether you are a Democrat or Republican, from a rural district or an urban one, part of the current majority or the minority, it is important to remember that representatives are elected by members of their district to be their voice in the House of Representatives.

As a leader, you have the added responsibility of representing your party. A political party is "an autonomous group of citizens having the purpose of making nominations and contesting elections in hope of gaining control over governmental power through the capture of public offices and the organization of the government."[1] In both the House of Representatives and the Senate, members elect leaders to "represent them on the floor, to advocate their policies and viewpoints, to coordinate their legislative efforts, and to help determine the schedule of legislative business."[2] Leaders are spokesmen and -women for their parties, as well as the Senate and the House nationally. The responsibilities that a leadership position entails may conflict with your role as representative from your district and/or your own political ideologies and personal philosophy.

Along with the other leaders of your party, you are responsible for holding your members together in accordance with the party platform. Here are excerpts from Republican and Democratic party platforms:

---

[1] *Political Parties in America*, by Robert Huckshorn, Monterey, CA: Brooks/Cole, 1984, p. 10.

[2] http://clerk.house.gov/member_info/memberfaq.aspx

This is a platform of enduring principle, not passing convenience—the product of the most open and transparent process in American political history. We offer it to our fellow Americans in the assurance that our Republican ideals are those that unify our country: Courage in the face of foreign foes. An optimistic patriotism, driven by a passion for freedom. Devotion to the inherent dignity and rights of every person. Faith in the virtues of self-reliance, civic commitment, and concern for one another. Distrust of government's interference in people's lives. Dedication to a rule of law that both protects and preserves liberty. ...

Our party embodies a uniquely American spirit. It is the spirit of independent minds, the conviction that open and honest debate is essential to the freedom we enjoy as Americans. This platform is a testament to that freedom and stands as our promise to future generations that we will do whatever it takes to preserve it. It is grounded on our heartfelt belief that our principles, our policies, and our vision will lead our American family, not just through present dangers, but to a horizon of prosperity and liberty mankind has only begun to explore.[3]

Democrats

Our party was founded on the conviction that wealth and privilege shouldn't be an entitlement to rule and the belief that the values of hardworking families are the values that should guide us.

We didn't become the most prosperous country in the world by rewarding greed and recklessness or by letting those with the most influence write their own rules. We got here by rewarding hard work and responsibility, by investing in people, and by growing our country from the bottom up.

Today Democrats are fighting to repair a decade of damage and grow an economy based on the values of Main Street, not greed and reckless speculation. Democrats are focused on rescuing our economy not just in the short run but also rebuilding our economy for the long run—an economy that lifts up not just some Americans, but all Americans.[4]

As a leader, you will also serve as an adviser to your colleagues, work with leaders from the opposing party as a consensus builder, mediate and negotiate deals among

---

[3] http://www.gop.com/2008Platform/2008platform.pdf

[4] http://www.democrats.org/about/our_party

representatives, and monitor the progress of legislation as it works its way through the committees.

MAJORITY LEADERSHIP

Speaker of the House: As a top leader of the majority party and the administrator in charge of the House of Representatives, you play a key role in the legislative process. In Mock Congress you are responsible for the following tasks:

1. Working with leaders from the opposing party;
2. Providing guidance and leadership to representatives from your party to help carry out the party's agenda;
3. Receiving all of the bills that pass out of committee with their accompanying rules and scheduling them on the calendar (this should be done in consultation with the other leaders of your party);
4. Presiding over the House during full floor debate (see the floor debate instructions in this workbook).

Majority Leader: As part of the majority leadership team, you assist the speaker and the whip with holding your caucus together, using a host of incentives and negotiating tactics. You should know the representatives in your party, their committees, their districts, their concerns, and provide them with guidance and leadership on decisions. Together, the leadership team should closely monitor the progress of all bills as they work their way through the committees.

Majority Whip: As part of the majority leadership team, you assist the speaker and the majority leader with holding your caucus together, using a host of incentives and negotiating tactics. Together, the leadership team should closely monitor the progress of all bills as they work their way through the committees. "The term 'whip' comes from the British hunting term 'whipper-in,' the person who keeps hounds from straying in a fox hunt."[5] In other words, count votes, craft political strategies, and communicate among your peers!

MINORITY LEADERSHIP

Minority Leader: As part of the minority leadership team, you are the top-ranking member of the minority party. You work to hold your caucus

---

[5] *American Government and Politics* by Joseph M. Bessette and John J. Pitney Jr., Wadsworth 2010, p. 398.

together, using a host of incentives and negotiating tactics. You should know the representatives in your party, their committees, their districts, their concerns, and provide them with guidance and leadership on all decisions. Furthermore, you should work closely with leaders from the opposing party. Together with the minority whip, you must monitor the progress of all bills as they work their way through the committees. While you don't work from the same position of strength as the majority leadership, you have a strong ability to influence the legislative process.

Minority Whip: As part of the minority leadership team, you assist the minority leader with holding your caucus together, using a host of incentives and negotiating tactics. Together, the leadership should closely monitor the progress of all bills as they work their way through the committees. "The term 'whip' comes from the British hunting term 'whipper-in,' the person who keeps hounds from straying in a fox hunt."[6] In other words, count votes, craft political strategies, and communicate among your peers!

ADVICE

- Remain in character during the simulation. Even if the beliefs of the representative you have been assigned differ from your own, challenge yourself to play the role. This will afford you the opportunity to see things from an alternative perspective.
- Be creative! The more fun you have, the more fun it is for everyone. Prepare, bring in information, and contribute something unique to the simulation.
- You are not assigned to a committee. This gives you the ability to float from committee to committee. You do not have a vote in any committee.
- You may not be able to get a compromise if you approach a single bill or a single aspect of a bill at a time.
- Work closely with the other leaders from your own political party and the leaders from the other political party. Your ability to work out compromises can set the tone for members of your party.
- Remember to think about what perspective someone else is speaking from—lobbyists, other representatives, leadership, etc. What are their goals? How do they differ from yours? Is there any overlap?
- Keep track of the progress of legislation in all four committees and know where the members of your party are with regard to each piece of legislation.
- Be respectful.

---

[6] *Ibid.*

Lobbyist Instructions

Note: in part 3 of the Simulation (floor debate) you will take on your voting role, acting as your assigned representative (see list of participants).

A company, organization, or other type of interest group has hired you to conduct what is known as lobbying. An interest group is:

> … an organization of people with shared goals that tries to influence public policy through a variety of activities. Every individual has interests, and interest groups are a mechanism for people with shared goals to protect or advance their own interests. People can try to influence government on their own—such as by calling or writing their elected representatives to voice their opinion, or by voting in an election. Another way that people can influence government is by joining a group that is organized to accomplish an objective.[1]

"Lobbying" is one way that interest groups try to influence government, and government officials more specifically. Inside lobbyists are professionals who work inside the capital, meeting with lawmakers and their legislative staff. By providing expert information and insight, they attempt to sway officials' votes and/or opinions. "Lobbyists communicate with public officials in many different ways, including formal presentations, written memos and policy papers, informal emails or notes, face-to-face

---

[1] *American Government: Historical, Popular and Global Perspectives* by Kenneth Dautrich and David Yalof. Boston: Wadsworth, 2009, p. 326.

meetings, or informal discussions over a meal or drink."[2] A good lobbyist provides quality information in the form of persuasive arguments. In this respect, contemporary members of congress may even rely on lobbyists when they have to make decisions on a particular topic.[3]

Lobbyists may not bribe public officials: "A Member or employee of the House may not accept a gift of any value from a registered lobbyist, an organization that employs a registered lobbyist or an agent of a foreign principal."[4] Therefore, do your homework! Armed with data, relevant information and charm, you may be able to successfully convince legislators to agree with your perspective. Of course, as a lobbyist, you have an added incentive to do so, because your own livelihood is dependent upon your success.

Below are the four lobbyist positions and the bills that each has been asked to focus their attention upon. The U.S. Chamber of Commerce and the National Education Association represent two of the most influential interest groups in the nation. While you should attempt to accomplish the stated goals while the bills are in committee, be prepared that you will not be successful. Therefore, do not limit your lobbying efforts only to members of certain committees. If a bill that you are opposed to passes out of committee, you can still lay the groundwork for it to die on the floor.

LOBBYIST 1: AMERICAN CIVIL LIBERTIES UNION

Bill 1 H.R. 1526 Drone Aircraft Privacy and Transparency Act of 2017. *Lobbying in favor of this bill.*

Bill 7 H.R. 83 Mobilizing Against Sanctuary Cities. *Lobbying in opposition to this bill.*

Bill 8 H.R. 2437 Back the Blue Act of 2017. *Lobbying in opposition to this bill.*

LOBBYIST 2: CHAMBER OF COMMERCE

Bill 2 H.R. 2479 Leading Infrastructure for Tomorrow's America Act. *Lobbying in favor of Title I of this bill.*

Bill 4. H.R. 15 Raise the Wage Act. *Lobbying in opposition to this bill.*

Bill 5. H.R. 2272 COAST Anti-Drilling Act. *Lobbying in opposition to this bill.*

---

[2] *Ibid., p. 343.*

[3] *Ibid., p. 343.*

[4] http://www.cleanupwashington.org/lobbying/page.cfm?pageid=43

LOBBYIST 3: SIERRA CLUB

Bill 2 H.R. 2479 Leading Infrastructure for Tomorrow's America Act. *Lobbying in favor of Title III, Sec. V of this bill.*

Bill 5 H.R. 2272 COAST Anti-Drilling Act. *Lobbying in favor of this bill.*

Bill 6 H.R. 2695 Environmental Justice Small Grants Program Act of 2017. *Lobbying in favor of this bill.*

LOBBYIST 4: NATIONAL EDUCATION ASSOCIATION

Bill 2 H.R. 2479 Leading Infrastructure for Tomorrow's America Act. *Lobbying in favor of Title III, Sec. VI of this bill.*

Bill 3 H.R. 610 Choices in Education Act of 2017. *Lobbying in opposition to this bill.*

Bill 4 H.R. 15 Raise the Wage Act. *Lobbying in favor of this bill.*

ADVICE

- Remain in character during the simulation. Even if the beliefs of the lobbyist you have been assigned differ from your own, challenge yourself to play the role. This will afford you the opportunity to see things from an alternative perspective.
- Be creative! The more fun you have, the more fun it is for everyone. Prepare, bring in information, and contribute something unique to the simulation.
- You are not a member of Congress. This gives you the ability to float from committee to committee, representative to representative.
- Know the representatives who will be amenable to your position and whose minds you need to change. Have a plan of attack—work your way systematically through meetings with as many representatives as you can.
- In order to meet with representatives, politely ask if they would be willing to speak with you for a few minutes alone (or in a small group). Preferably do so outside of committee in the classroom or in the hallway. Introduce yourself and be personable. Explain your position and your reason for it.
- It is important that you not be perceived as annoying or aggressive (though you may have to be aggressive to ensure that you have the access necessary to do your job).
- Work closely with the leaders of both political parties if you are able.
- Do not be rude to the other lobbyists or be too intrusive during the hearings.
- You may not ask questions of the witnesses during committee hearings.
- Remember to think about what perspective someone else is speaking from. What are their goals? How do they differ from yours? Is there any overlap?
- Keep track of the progress of legislation in all four committees, and know where representatives are with regard to each piece of legislation.
- Be respectful.

Witness Instructions

Note: after giving testimony, you will take on your post-witness role, acting as your assigned representative (see list of participants).

About Your Role

Representatives hold hearings in order to hear from a range of individuals (witnesses) while preparing to work on legislation.

> A hearing is a meeting or session of a Senate, House, Joint, or Special Committee of Congress, usually open to the public, to obtain information and opinions on proposed legislation, conduct an investigation, or evaluate/ oversee the activities of a government department or the implementation of a Federal law. In addition, hearings may also be purely exploratory in nature, providing testimony and data about topics of current interest. Most Congressional hearings are published two months to two years after they are held.[1]

Hearings also allow interested individuals and groups who may be affected by public laws the opportunity to provide input. Congressional scholar Walter J. Oleszek wrote the following about the importance of the hearing process: "The decision to hold hearings is often a critical point in the life of a bill. Measures brought to the floor without

---

[1] http://www.gpoaccess.gov/chearings/index.html

first being the subject of hearings are likely to be the targets of sharp criticism. ... The sanctity of the committee stage is based on the assumption that the experts—the committee members—carefully scrutinized a proposal, and hearings provide a demonstrable record of that scrutiny."[2] Potential witnesses are carefully chosen and reviewed by the committee. Only those invited by the committee are allowed to testify. The format of testimony, order of witnesses, and the nature and order of the questions are all carefully determined in advance.[3]

In Mock Congress, each committee will hold one hearing, where they will hear from two witnesses. In the simulation, each witness will play two different roles. Your job is to represent each role as realistically and intelligently as possible.

You will research the bills that you will be testifying about, think about the kinds of questions that representatives may ask, and prepare talking points in advance. Your job is not necessarily to change minds or to sway representatives to your way of thinking—your job is to provide honest information from your position. Your testimony may help the committee "mark up" (or alter) the bill. Below is a description of the roles each witness will play.

NOTE: When you finish testifying before both committees, you will no longer be playing the role of a witness. At this point in the simulation, take on the secondary role of a representative so that you may participate (briefly) in committee work (see Full List of Participants in this workbook for your secondary role). You will participate in the remainder of the simulation as a representative. Upon learning what bills have passed out of committee, you should prepare arguments for or against each bill like the rest of the representatives.

WITNESS A

*You will testify in these two roles before two different committees in the order they are listed.

Role 1: You are a Senior Education Policy Specialist with the National Conference of State Legislatures. **You will testify before the Education and the Workforce Committee regarding Bill 3 (H.R. 610 Choices in Education Act of 2017).** You present information on the history and adoption of school vouchers in the various fifty states. In addition you present statistics on whether vouchers increase access to quality education and services as well as the effects of vouchers on students' academic achievements.

Role 2: You are the Director of the U.S. Fish and Wildlife Agency. You seek to eliminate, or at least reduce future drilling off the coast of the United States. You discuss

_____

[2] http://lieberman.senate.gov/assets/pdf/crs/senatehearings.pdf
[3] *Ibid.*

the environmental impact of oil spills on ecosystems and human health and explain what's at stake if the outer continental shelf is not protected. **You will testify before the Natural Resources Committee in strong support of Bill 5 (H.R. 2272 COAST Anti-Drilling Act).**

WITNESS B

*You will testify in these two roles before two different committees in the order they are listed.

Role 1: You are an oil and gas well drilling expert. **You will testify before the Natural Resources Committee regarding Bill 5 (H.R. 2272 COAST Anti-Drilling Act)** that contemporary drilling practices are safe but not 100% preventable. Drilling means jobs for Americans and reduces our dependence on foreign oil. You believe that offshore drilling is not dangerous and is beneficial for the United States financially and politically.

Role 2: You serve as Co-Chair of the National Coalition for Public Education. **You will testify before the Education and the Workforce Committee against Bill 3 (H.R. 610 Choices in Education Act of 2017).** You discuss various facts and statistics about private school vouchers including their impact on public schools and whether they offer parents real choice. You believe this bill harms public schools, threatens their financial stability, and reduces student access to crucial services.

WITNESS C

*You will testify in these two roles before two different committees in the order they are listed.

Role 1: You are the Executive Director of the Electronic Privacy Information Center in Washington, DC. **You will testify before the Transportation and Infrastructure Committee in support of Bill 1 (H.R. 1526 The Drone Aircraft Privacy and Transparency Act of 2017).** Despite their benefits, you believe that unmanned aircraft systems present new challenges, including safety and privacy concerns. You provide information on existing laws pertaining to drone use, outline specific privacy concerns, and stress the need for increased privacy regulations. You believe that this bill is an excellent first step to a more comprehensive plan for drone deployment in the United States.

Role 2: You are the Executive Director of the United States Conference of Mayors. **You will testify before the House Judiciary Committee against Bill 7 (H.R. 83 Mobilizing Against Sanctuary Cities),** which you believe will undermine relationships of trust between immigrant communities and local police departments. After describing your organization, you present statistics on economic growth and crime rates in sanctuary cities and provide an assessment of the effects this bill will have on local law enforcement agencies. In concluding, you suggest alternative ways to ensure public safety without undermining police-community relations.

WITNESS D

*You will testify in these two roles before two different committees in the order they are listed.

Role 1: You are the Acting Director of U.S. Immigration and Customs Enforcement. **You will testify before the Judiciary Committee in support of Bill 7 (H.R. 83 Mobilizing Against Sanctuary Cities).** You discuss your agency's mission, provide the most recent data on the number of detainers issued by ICE (including the notable criminal activity associated with these detainers), and lay out some of the problems when law enforcement agencies fail to honor immigration detainers. Overall, you make the case that this bill will strengthen national security and help make sanctuary cities safer.

Role 2: You are a Research Fellow at the Brookings Institute's Center for Technology Innovation. **You will testify before the Transportation and Infrastructure Committee with respect to Bill 1 (H.R. 1526 The Drone Aircraft Privacy and Transparency Act of 2017).** You identify some of the top non-military uses of unmanned aircraft systems and their potential benefits. Although there are important privacy issues at stake, you believe existing laws adequately protect people's privacy and that additional legislation is unnecessary and could potentially stifle innovation and economic growth.

ADVICE

- Introduce yourself when you arrive before the committee, and make sure all members of the committee can hear you.
- Remain in character during the simulation. Even if the beliefs of the witnesses you have been assigned differ from your own, challenge yourself to play the roles. This will afford you the opportunity to see things from an alternative perspective.
- Be creative! The more fun you have, the more fun it is for everyone. Prepare, bring in information, and contribute something unique to the simulation.
- You can bring notes with you. Do your best to respond to questions as best you can, based on what you learned in doing your research. If you don't know the exact answer to a question, say so, or respond with relevant information that you do know. Representatives, leaders, or lobbyists must not persuade you to change your beliefs!

- During your testimony, the representatives should be giving you their full attention. If the chair is not doing an adequate job of maintaining control over the hearing process, let the instructor know.
- During the simulation, lobbyists may be distracting some of the representatives. Do your best to not lose focus. However, lobbyists may not ask questions of the witnesses or interject their opinion during committee hearings.
- Be respectful.

Quick Reference Bills

Bills Being Considered in Committee, Experts Who Will be Testifying, Identified Lobbyists

1. H.R.1526 Drone Aircraft Privacy and Transparency Act of 2017.

Drone Aircraft Privacy and Transparency Act of 2017 – Places restrictions on the licensing of unmanned aircraft systems, including for law enforcement or intelligence purposes.

Committee: Transportation and Infrastructure
Expert Testimony: (1) Executive Director of the Electronic Privacy Information Center; (2) Research Fellow at the Brookings Institute's Center for Technology Innovation
Lobbyists: ACLU

2. H.R.2479 Leading Infrastructure for Tomorrow's America Act

Leading Infrastructure for Tomorrow's Act – provides $40 billion to deploy secure and resilient broadband, reauthorizes the Diesel Emissions Reductions Act, and provides $5 million for energy efficiency improvements at public school facilities.

Committee: Transportation and Infrastructure
Lobbyists: (1) Sierra Club; (2) Chamber of Commerce; (3) National Education Association

3. H.R.610 Choices in Education Act of 2017

Choices in Education Act of 2017 – Repeals the Elementary and Secondary Education Act of 1965 and establishes an education voucher program.

Committee: Education and the Workforce
Expert Testimony: (1) Senior Education Policy Specialist with the National Conference of State Legislatures; (2) Co-Chair of the National Coalition for Public Education
Lobbyists: (1) National Education Association

4. H.R.15 Raise the Wage Act

Raise the Wage Act – Raises the minimum wage to $15 per hour by 2024, including the tipped-minimum wage and wages for workers under the age of twenty.

Committee: Education and the Workforce
Lobbyists: (1) National Education Association; (2) Chamber of Commerce (Labor, Immigration, and Employee Benefits Division)

5. H.R.2272 Clean Ocean and Safe Tourism Anti-Drilling Act

Clean Ocean and Safe Tourism Anti-Drilling Act, or the COAST Anti-Drilling Act – prohibits offshore oil and gas drilling in the Atlantic Ocean.

Committee: Natural Resources
Expert Testimony: (1) Oil and Gas Well Drilling Expert; (2) Director of the U.S. Fish and Wildlife Agency
Lobbyists: (1) Sierra Club; (2) Chamber of Commerce (Institute for 21st Century Energy)

6. H.R.2695 Environmental Justice Small Grants Program Act of 2017

Environmental Justice Small Grants Program Act of 2017 – establishes the Office of Environmental Justice in the Environment Protection Agency and authorizes an environmental justice small grants program.

Committee: Natural Resources
Lobbyists: (1) Sierra Club

7. H.R. 83 Mobilizing Against Sanctuary Cities Act

Mobilizing Against Sanctuary Cities Act – stops all federal funds from going to states or localities which resist or ban enforcement of federal immigration laws, or refuse to cooperate with immigration officials.

Committee: Judiciary
Expert Testimony: (1) Acting Director of U.S. Immigration and Customs Enforcement; (2) Executive Director of the United States Conference of Mayors
Lobbyists: American Civil Liberties Union

8. H.R.2437 Back the Blue Act of 2017

Back the Blue Act of 2017 – Establishes a mandatory minimum sentence of ten years in prison for offenders who kill, or attempt to kill, law enforcement officers. Offenders are subject to thirty years in prison or the death penalty if death results.
Committee: Transportation and Infrastructure

Committee: Judiciary
Lobbyists: ACLU

House Committee on Transportation and Infrastructure Bill 1

Title: H.R. 1526 Drone Aircraft Privacy and Transparency Act of 2017

Sponsor: Representative Peter Welch [VT-At Large] (introduced 3/13/2017)

Summary: Prohibits the Secretary of Transportation from approving, issuing, or awarding any certificate, license, or other grant of authority to operate a drone system in the national airspace system unless the application for it includes a data collection statement, meeting certain requirements, that provides reasonable assurance that the applicant will operate the drone system in accordance with privacy principles. Applies the same privacy principles to law enforcement agencies which may not use an unmanned aircraft system for law enforcement or intelligence purposes, except pursuant to a warrant.

FULL TEXT:

A BILL

To amend the FAA Modernization and Reform Act of 2012 to provide guidance and limitations regarding the integration of unmanned aircraft systems into United States airspace, and for other purposes.

Be it enacted by the Senate and House of Representatives of the United States of America in Congress assembled,

SECTION 1. SHORT TITLE.

This Act may be cited as the "Drone Aircraft Privacy and Transparency Act of 2017".

SEC. 3 GUIDANCE AND LIMITATIONS REGARDING UNMANNED AIRCRAFT SYSTEMS

(a) IN GENERAL.—Subtitle B of title III of the FAA Modernization and Reform Act of 2012 is amended by adding at the end the following new sections:

SEC. 338. DATA COLLECTION STATEMENTS

"(a) IN GENERAL.—Beginning on the date of the enactment of this section, the Secretary of Transportation may not approve, issue, or award any certificate, license, or other grant of authority to operate an unmanned aircraft system in the national airspace system unless the application for such certificate, license, or other grant of authority includes—

"(1) a data collection statement in accordance with the requirements of subsection (b) that provides reasonable assurance that the applicant will operate the unmanned aircraft system in accordance with the privacy principles;

(b) DATA COLLECTION STATEMENT.—A data collection statement under subsection (a), with respect to an unmanned aircraft system, shall include information identifying—

"(1) the individuals or entities that will have the power to use the unmanned aircraft system;

"(2) the specific locations in which the unmanned aircraft system will operate;

"(3) the maximum period for which the unmanned aircraft system will operate in each flight;

"(4) whether the unmanned aircraft system will collect information or data about individuals or groups of individuals, and if so—

"(A) the circumstances under which the system will be used; and

"(B) the specific kinds of information or data the system will collect about individuals or groups of individuals and how such information or data, as well as conclusions drawn from such information or data, will be used, disclosed, and otherwise handled, including—

"(i) how the collection or retention of such information or data that is unrelated to the specified use will be minimized;

"(ii) whether such information or data might be sold, leased, or otherwise provided to third parties, and if so, under what circumstances it might be so sold or leased;

"(iii) the period for which such information or data will be retained; and "(iv) when and how such information or data, including information or data no longer relevant to the specified use, will be destroyed;

"(5) the possible impact the operation of the unmanned aircraft system may have upon the privacy of individuals;

"(6) the specific steps that will be taken to mitigate any possible impact identified under paragraph (5), including steps to protect against unauthorized disclosure of any information or data described in paragraph (4), such as the use of encryption methods and other security features that will be used;

"(7) a telephone number or electronic mail address that an individual with complaints about the operation of the unmanned aircraft system may use to report such complaints and to request confirmation that personally identifiable data relating to such individual has been collected;

"(8) in a case in which personally identifiable data relating to an individual has been collected, a reasonable process for the individual to request to obtain such data in a timely and an intelligible manner;

"(9) in a case in which a request described in paragraph (8) is denied, a process by which the individual may obtain the reasons for the denial and challenge the denial; and

"(10) in a case in which personally identifiable data relating to an individual has been collected, a process by which the individual may challenge the accuracy of such data and, if the challenge is successful, have such data erased or amended.

SEC. 340. WARRANTS REQUIRED FOR GENERALIZED SURVEILLANCE

"(a) IN GENERAL.—A governmental entity may not use an unmanned aircraft system or request information or data collected by another person using an unmanned aircraft system for protective activities, or for law enforcement or intelligence purposes, except pursuant to a warrant issued using the procedures described in the Federal Rules of Criminal Procedure (or, in the case of a State court, issued using State warrant procedures) by a court of competent jurisdiction, or as permitted under the Foreign Intelligence Surveillance Act of 1978.

"(b) EXCEPTIONS.—

"(1) IN GENERAL.—Subsection (a) shall not apply in a case in which a governmental entity is using an unmanned aircraft system in exigent circumstances (as defined in paragraph (2)).

"(2) EXIGENT CIRCUMSTANCES DEFINED.—Exigent circumstances exist when—

"(A) a law enforcement entity reasonably believes there is an imminent danger of death or serious physical injury; or

"(B) a law enforcement entity reasonably believes there is a high risk of an imminent terrorist attack by a specific individual or organization and the Secretary of Homeland Security has determined that credible intelligence indicates there is such a risk.

"(c) PROHIBITION ON USE AS EVIDENCE.—If information has been collected by means of use of an unmanned aircraft system, no part of the contents of that information and no evidence derived from that information may be received in evidence in any trial, hearing, or other proceeding in or before any court, grand jury, department, officer, agency, regulatory body, legislative committee, or other authority of the United States, a State, or a political subdivision thereof unless that information is collected in accordance with this section.

"(e) INJUNCTION.—A person injured by an act in violation of this section may bring in an appropriate State court or an appropriate district court of the United States an action to enjoin such violation."

House Committee on Transportation and Infrastructure Bill 2

Title: H.R. 2479 Leading Infrastructure for Tomorrow's America Act

Sponsor: Representative Frank Pallone [NJ-6] (introduced 5/17/2017)

Summary: Provides $40 billion over five years to expand access to broadband internet. Three quarters of this funding will be used to deploy broadband in unserved areas of the country. The remaining funds will be given to states.

Reauthorizes the Diesel Emissions Reductions Act, providing $1 billion over five years to reduce emissions from older vehicles including school buses.

Provides $5 million over five years for energy efficiency improvements and renewable energy improvements at public school facilities.

FULL TEXT

A BILL

To rebuild and modernize the Nation's infrastructure to expand access to broadband internet and modernize the energy supply infrastructure

Be it enacted by the Senate and House of Representatives of the United States of America in Congress assembled,

SECTION 1. SHORT TITLE

(a) SHORT TITLE.—This Act may be cited as the "Leading Infrastructure for Tomorrow's America Act".

TITLE I—EXPANSION OF BROADBAND ACCESS

Section 10001. **EXPANSION OF BROADBAND ACCESS.**

(a) PROGRAM ESTABLISHED.—The Assistant Secretary shall establish a program to expand access to broadband for communities throughout the United States in a manner that protects consumer privacy and promotes network security.

(b) USE OF PROGRAM FUNDS.—

(1) DEPLOYMENT OF BROADBAND THROUGH NATIONAL REVERSE AUCTION.—Of the amounts authorized for the program, 75 percent shall be distributed by the Assistant Secretary to private entities to deploy broadband in unserved areas of the United States through a national reverse auction.

(2) DEPLOYMENT OF BROADBAND THROUGH STATES.—Of the amounts authorized for the program, 25 percent shall be distributed by the Assistant Secretary among the States for the States to distribute to private entities (or governmental entities for the deployment of Next Generation 9-1-1 services) through a statewide reverse auction in accordance with the program and project requirements described in this section—

(A) to deploy broadband in unserved areas; or

(B) if a State does not have an unserved area, to—

(i) deploy broadband in underserved areas;

(ii) deploy broadband or connective technology to a school or library that does not receive funding under subpart F of part 54 of title 47, Code of Federal Regulations; or

(iii) fund the deployment of Next Generation 9-1-1 services.

(c) PROGRAM REQUIREMENTS.—

(1) TECHNOLOGY NEUTRALITY REQUIRED.—Any funds distributed under the program shall not favor a project using any particular technology.

(2) MATCHING FUNDS PREFERENCE.—There shall be a preference under the program for projects with at least 50 percent matching funds from the private sector.

(h) AUTHORIZATION OF APPROPRIATIONS.—There is authorized to be appropriated to the Assistant Secretary $40,000,000,000 for fiscal years 2018 through 2022 to carry out the program described in subsection (a), and such amount is authorized to remain available until expended.

TITLE III—CLEAN ENERGY INFRASTRUCTURE

PART 5—DIESEL EMISSIONS REDUCTION

Sec. 32501. **Short Title**

This part may be cited as the "Diesel Emissions Reduction Act of 2017".

Sec. 32502. **Reauthorization of Diesel Emissions**

Section 797(a) of the Energy Policy Act of 2005 is amended—

(1) by striking "$100,000,000" and inserting "$200,000,000"; and

(2) by striking "2016" and inserting "2022".

PART 6—ENERGY IMPROVEMENTS AT PUBLIC SCHOOL FACILITIES

Sec 32601. **Grants for Energy Efficency Improvements and Renewable Energy Improvements at Public School Facilities**

(a) DEFINITIONS.—In this section:

ENERGY IMPROVEMENTS.—The term "energy improvements" means—

(A) any improvement, repair, or renovation, to a school that will result in a direct reduction in school energy costs including but not limited to improvements to building envelope, air conditioning, ventilation, heating system, domestic hot water heating, compressed air systems, distribution systems, lighting, power systems and controls;

(B) any improvement, repair, renovation, or installation that leads to an improvement in teacher and student health including but not limited to indoor air quality, daylighting, ventilation, electrical lighting, and acoustics; and

(C) the installation of renewable energy technologies (such as wind power, photovoltaics, solar thermal systems, geothermal energy, hydrogen-fueled systems, biomass-based systems, biofuels, anaerobic digesters, and hydropower) involved in the improvement, repair, or renovation to a school.

(b) AUTHORITY.—From amounts made available for grants under this section, the Secretary of Energy shall provide competitive grants to eligible entities to make energy improvements authorized by this section.

(d) COMPETITIVE CRITERIA.—The competitive criteria used by the Secretary shall include the following:

(1) The fiscal capacity of the eligible entity to meet the needs for improvements of school facilities without assistance under this section, including the ability of the eligible entity to raise funds through the use of local bonding capacity and otherwise.

(2) The likelihood that the local educational agency or eligible entity will maintain, in good condition, any facility whose improvement is assisted.

(3) The potential energy efficiency and safety benefits from the proposed energy improvements.

(e) APPLICATIONS.—To be eligible to receive a grant under this section, an applicant must submit to the Secretary an application that includes each of the following:

(1) A needs assessment of the current condition of the school and facilities that are to receive the energy improvements.

(2) A draft work plan of what the applicant hopes to achieve at the school and a description of the energy improvements to be carried out.

(3) A description of the applicant's capacity to provide services and comprehensive support to make the energy improvements.

(4) An assessment of the applicant's expected needs for operation and maintenance training funds, and a plan for use of those funds, if any.

(5) An assessment of the expected energy efficiency and safety benefits of the energy improvements.

(6) A cost estimate of the proposed energy improvements.

(7) An identification of other resources that are available to carry out the activities for which funds are requested under this section, including the availability of utility programs and public benefit funds.

(f) USE OF GRANT AMOUNTS.—

(1) IN GENERAL.—The recipient of a grant under this section shall use the grant amounts only to make the energy improvements contemplated in the application, subject to the other provisions of this subsection.

(j) AUTHORIZATION OF APPROPRIATIONS.—There is authorized to be appropriated to carry out this section $100,000,000 for each of fiscal years 2018 through 2022.

House Committee on Education and the Workforce Bill 3

Title: H.R. 610 Choices in Education Act of 2017

Sponsor: Representative Steve King [IA-4] (introduced 1/23/2017)

Summary: This bill repeals the Elementary and Secondary Education Act of 1965 and limits the authority of the Department of Education (ED) such that ED is authorized only to award block grants to qualified states.

The bill establishes an education voucher program, through which each state shall distribute block grant funds among local educational agencies (LEAs) based on the number of eligible children within each LEA's geographical area. From these amounts, each LEA shall: (1) distribute a portion of funds to parents who elect to enroll their child in a private school or to home-school their child, and (2) do so in a manner that ensures that such payments will be used for appropriate educational expenses.

To be eligible to receive a block grant, a state must: (1) comply with education voucher program requirements, and (2) make it lawful for parents of an eligible child to elect to enroll their child in any public or private elementary or secondary school in the state or to home-school their child.

FULL TEXT:

A BILL

To distribute Federal funds for elementary and secondary education in the form of vouchers for eligible students.

Be it enacted by the Senate and House of Representatives of the United States of America in Congress assembled,

SEC. 101. SHORT TITLE

This title may be cited as the "Choices in Education Act of 2017".

SEC. 102. REPEAL OF ELEMENTARY AND SECONDARY EDUCATION ACT AND LIMITATION ON SECRETARIAL AUTHORITY

(a) REPEAL.—The Elementary and Secondary Education Act of 1965 is repealed.
(b) LIMITATION ON SECRETARIAL AUTHORITY.—The authority of the Secretary under this title is limited to evaluating State applications under section 104 and making payments to States under section 103. The Secretary shall not impose any further requirements on States with respect to elementary and secondary education beyond the requirements of this title.

SEC. 103. BLOCK GRANTS TO STATES

(a) GRANTS TO STATES.—From amounts appropriated to carry out this title for a fiscal year, the Secretary shall award grants (from allotments made under subsection (b)) to qualified States to enable such States to carry out an education voucher program under section 105.

SEC. 104. APPLICATION

(a) APPLICATION.—To be eligible to receive a grant under this title, a State shall submit an application to the Secretary that includes assurances that the State will—
  (1) comply with the requirements of section 105; and
  (2) make it lawful for parents of an eligible child to elect—

(A) to enroll their child in any public or private elementary or secondary school in the State; or

(B) to home-school their child.

SEC. 105. EDUCATION VOUCHER PROGRAM REQUIREMENTS

(a) EDUCATION VOUCHER PROGRAM.—

(1) IN GENERAL.—The State shall distribute funds received under this title among the local educational agencies in the State based on the number of eligible children enrolled in the public schools operated by each local educational agency and the number of eligible children within each local educational agency's geographical area whose parents elect to send their child to a private school or to home-school their child.

(2) SENSE OF CONGRESS.—It is the sense of Congress that States should distribute non-Federal funds for elementary and secondary education in a manner that promotes competition and choices in education.

(b) IDENTIFICATION OF ELIGIBLE CHILDREN; ALLOCATION AND DISTRIBUTION OF FUNDS.—

(1) IDENTIFICATION OF ELIGIBLE CHILDREN.—

(A) LEA IDENTIFICATION.—On an annual basis, on a date to be determined by the Secretary, each local educational agency shall inform the State educational agency of—

(i) the number of eligible children enrolled in public schools served by the local educational agency; and

(ii) the number of eligible children within each local educational agency's geographical area whose parents elect—

(I) to send their child to a private school; or

(II) to home-school their child.

(B) STATE IDENTIFICATION.—On an annual basis, on a date to be determined by the Secretary, each State educational agency shall inform the Secretary of the total number of children identified by all local educational agencies in the State under subparagraph (A).

(2) AMOUNT OF PAYMENT.—

(A) IN GENERAL.—Subject to subparagraph (B), the amount of payment for each eligible child in a State shall be equal to—

(i) the total amount allotted to the State under this title; divided by

(ii) the total number of eligible children in the State identified under paragraph (1).

(B) LIMITATIONS.—

(i) In the case of a payment made to the parent of an eligible child who elects to attend a private school, the amount of the payment described in subparagraph (A) for each eligible child shall not exceed the cost for tuition, fees, and transportation for the eligible child to attend the private school.

(ii) In the case of a payment made to a parent of an eligible child who elects to home-school such child, the amount of the payment described in subparagraph (A) for each eligible child shall not exceed the cost of home-schooling the child.

(3) ALLOCATION TO LOCAL EDUCATIONAL AGENCIES.—Based on the identification of eligible children in paragraph (1), the State educational agency shall provide to a local educational agency an amount equal to the product of—

(A) the amount available for each eligible child in the State, as determined in paragraph (2); multiplied by

(B) the number of eligible children identified by the local educational agency under paragraph (1)(A).

(4) DISTRIBUTION TO SCHOOLS.—From amounts allocated under paragraph (3), each local educational agency that receives funds under such paragraph shall distribute a portion of such funds to the public schools served by the local educational agency, which amount shall—

(A) be based on the number of eligible children enrolled in such schools and included in the count submitted under paragraph (1)(A); and

(B) be distributed in a manner that would, in the absence of such Federal funds, supplement the funds made available from non-Federal resources for the education of eligible children, and not to supplant such funds.

(5) DISTRIBUTION TO PARENTS.—

(A) IN GENERAL.—From the amounts allocated under paragraph (3), each local educational agency that receives funds under such paragraph shall distribute a portion of such funds, in an amount equal to the amount described in paragraph (2), to the parents of each eligible child within the local educational agency's geographical area who elect to send their child to a private school or to home-school their child (as the case may be) and whose child is included in the count of such eligible children under paragraph (1)(A), which amount shall be distributed in a manner so as to ensure that such payments will be used for appropriate educational expenses.

House Committee on Education and the Workforce Bill 4

Title: H.R. 15 Raise the Wage Act

Sponsor: Representative Robert C. "Bobby" Scott [VA-3] (introduced 5/25/2017)

Summary: Raises the minimum wage to $15 per hour by 2024. Thereafter, the value of the minimum wage is indexed to the median wage growth, preventing any erosion in the minimum wage's inflation-adjusted value.

During the first year of enactment, the bill raises the tipped-minimum wage from $2.13 to $4.15 an hour. For each succeeding year, the bill raises the subminimum wage for tipped workers by at least $1.15, until it reaches parity with the full minimum wage.

The bill phases out the youth minimum wage. During the first year of enactment, the bill increases youth wages from $4.25 to $5.00 an hour. For each succeeding year, the youth wage will increase at least $1.05, until the youth wage equals the federal minimum wage.

FULL TEXT:

A BILL

To provide for increases in the Federal minimum wage, and for other purposes.

Be it enacted by the Senate and House of Representatives of the United States of America in Congress assembled,

SECTION 1. SHORT TITLE

This Act may be cited as the "Raise the Wage Act".

SEC. 2. MINIMUM WAGE INCREASES

(a) IN GENERAL.—Section 6(a)(1) of the Fair Labor Standards Act of 1938 is amended to read as follows:

"(1) except as otherwise provided in this section, not less than—

"(A) $9.25 an hour, beginning on the effective date under section 7 of the Raise the Wage Act;

"(B) $10.10 an hour, beginning 1 year after such effective date;

"(C) $11.00 an hour, beginning 2 years after such effective date;

"(D) $12.00 an hour, beginning 3 years after such effective date;

"(E) $13.00 an hour, beginning 4 years after such effective date;

"(F) $13.50 an hour, beginning 5 years after such effective date;

"(G) $14.25 an hour, beginning 6 years after such effective date;

"(H) $15.00 an hour, beginning 7 years after such effective date; and

"(I) beginning on the date that is 8 years after such effective date, and annually thereafter, the amount determined by the Secretary under subsection (h);".

(b) DETERMINATION BASED ON INCREASE IN THE MEDIAN HOURLY WAGE OF ALL EMPLOYEES.—Section 6 of the Fair Labor Standards Act of 1938 is amended by adding at the end the following:

"(h)(1) Not later than each date that is 90 days before a new minimum wage determined under subsection (a)(1)(I) is to take effect, the Secretary shall determine the minimum wage to be in effect under this subsection for each period described in subsection (a)(1)(I). The wage determined under this subsection for a year shall be—

"(A) not less than the amount in effect under subsection (a)(1) on the date of such determination;

"(B) increased from such amount by the annual percentage increase, if any, in the median hourly wage of all employees as determined by the Bureau of Labor Statistics; and

"(C) rounded to the nearest multiple of $0.05.

"(2) In calculating the annual percentage increase in the median hourly wage of all employees for purposes of paragraph (1)(B), the Secretary, through the Bureau of Labor Statistics, shall compile data on the hourly wages of all employees to determine such a median hourly wage and compare such median hourly wage for the most recent year for which data are available with the median hourly wage determined for the preceding year."

SEC. 3. TIPPED EMPLOYEES

(a) BASE MINIMUM WAGE FOR TIPPED EMPLOYEES.—Section 3(m)(1) of the Fair Labor Standards Act of 1938 is amended to read as follows:

"(1) the cash wage paid such employee, which for purposes of such determination shall be not less than—

"(A) for the 1-year period beginning on the effective date under section 7 of the Raise the Wage Act, $4.15 an hour;

"(B) for each succeeding 1-year period until the hourly wage under this paragraph equals the wage in effect under section 6(a)(1) for such period, an hourly wage equal to the amount determined under this paragraph for the preceding year, increased by the lesser of—

i) $1.15; or

"(ii) the amount necessary for the wage in effect under this paragraph to equal the wage in effect under section 6(a)(1) for such period, rounded to the nearest multiple of $0.05; and

"(C) for each succeeding 1-year period after the increase made pursuant to subparagraph (B)(ii), the minimum wage in effect under section 6(a)(1)

SEC. 4. NEWLY HIRED EMPLOYEES WHO ARE LESS THAN 20 YEARS OLD

(a) BASE MINIMUM WAGE FOR NEWLY HIRED EMPLOYEES WHO ARE LESS THAN 20 YEARS OLD.—Section 6(g)(1) of the Fair Labor Standards Act of 1938 is amended by striking "a wage which is not less than $4.25 an hour." and inserting the following: "a wage at a rate that is not less than—

"(A) for the 1-year period beginning on the effective date under section 7 of the Raise the Wage Act, $5.00 an hour;

"(B) for each succeeding 1-year period until the hourly wage under this paragraph equals the wage in effect under section 6(a)(1) for such period, an hourly wage equal to the amount determined under this paragraph for the preceding year, increased by the lesser of—

"(i) $1.05; or

"(ii) the amount necessary for the wage in effect under this paragraph to equal the wage in effect under section 6(a)(1) for such period, rounded to the nearest multiple of $0.05; and

"(C) for each succeeding 1-year period after the increase made pursuant to subparagraph (B)(ii), the minimum wage in effect under section 6(a)(1)."

House Committee on Natural Resources Bill 5

Title: H.R. 2272 Clean Ocean and Safe Tourism (COAST) Anti-Drilling Act

Sponsor: Representative Frank Pallone [NJ-6] (introduced 05/01/2017)

Summary: Prohibits offshore oil and gas drilling in the Atlantic Ocean.

FULL TEXT:

A BILL

To amend the Outer Continental Shelf Lands Act to permanently prohibit the conduct of offshore drilling on the outer Continental Shelf in the Mid-Atlantic, South Atlantic, North Atlantic, and Straits of Florida planning areas.

Be it enacted by the Senate and House of Representatives of the United States of America in Congress assembled,

SECTION 1. SHORT TITLE.

This Act may be cited as the "Clean Ocean and Safe Tourism Anti-Drilling Act" or the "COAST Anti-Drilling Act".

SEC. 2. PROHIBITION OF OIL AND GAS LEASING IN CERTAIN AREAS OF THE OUTER CONTINENTAL SHELF.

Section 8 of the Outer Continental Shelf Lands Act is amended by adding at the end the following:

"(q) PROHIBITION OF OIL AND GAS LEASING IN CERTAIN AREAS OF THE OUTER CONTINENTAL SHELF.—Notwithstanding any other provision of this section or any other law, the Secretary of the Interior shall not issue a lease or any other authorization for the exploration, development, or production of oil, natural gas, or any other mineral in—

"(1) the Mid-Atlantic planning area;

"(2) the South Atlantic planning area;

"(3) the North Atlantic planning area; or

"(4) the Straits of Florida planning area.".

House Committee on Natural Resources Bill 6

Title: H.R. 2695 Environmental Justice Small Grants Program Act of 2017

Sponsor: Representative Pramila Jayapal [WA-7] (introduced 05/25/2017)

Summary: This bill establishes the Office of Environmental Justice in the Environment Protection Agency, which will be headed by a Director. The Director can make a grant, in an amount not to exceed $50,000, to an eligible entity to carry out an environmental justice project. Upon enactment, the bill authorizes a $16,000,000 appropriation for each fiscal year.

Full Text:

A BILL

To establish an Office of Environmental Justice in the Environmental Protection Agency and to authorize an environmental justice small grants program, and for other purposes.

Be it enacted by the Senate and House of Representatives of the United States of America in Congress assembled,

SECTION 1: SHORT TITLE

This Act may be cited as the "Environmental Justice Small Grants Program Act of 2017".

SEC 2. FINDINGS

Congress finds the following:

(1) Despite Executive Order 12898 (relating to "Federal Actions to Address Environmental Justice in Minority Populations and Low-Income Populations"), communities of color, low income communities, people with limited English proficiency, indigenous peoples, and people living with disabilities experience the impacts of climate change at a disproportionate rate.

(2) The Environmental Protection Agency formed the Environmental Justice Small Grants Program to support and empower frontline communities that are working on solutions to the disproportionate impacts of climate change.

(3) Between 2000 and 2015, the Environmental Protection Agency, through the Environmental Justice Small Grants Program, awarded more than 630 small grants to assist with the cost of conducting research and education, as well as developing community-based solutions.

SEC. 3. OFFICE OF ENVIRONMENTAL JUSTICE

There is established in the Environmental Protection Agency an Office of Environmental Justice, which shall be headed by a Director.

SEC. 4. ENVIORNMENTAL JUSTICE SMALL GRANTS PROGRAM.

(a) IN GENERAL.—The Director of the Office of Environmental Justice shall establish an environmental justice grant program to make grants to eligible entities in accordance with this section.

(b) GRANTS.—The Director may make a grant under this section, in an amount not to exceed $50,000, to an eligible entity to carry out an environmental justice project.

(c) DEFINITIONS.—In this section:

    (1) AFFECTED COMMUNITY.—The term "affected community" means a community that—

        (A) may be disproportionately affected by environmental harms and risks; and

        (B) is affected by a local environmental or public health issue that is identified in an application for a grant under this section.

    (2) ELIGIBLE ENTITY.—The term "eligible entity" means—

        (A) an entity that—

            (i) is an organization (including an environmental justice network, a faith-based organization, or non-profit organization;

            (ii) demonstrates that it has worked directly with the affected community, as determined by the Director;

        (B) a federally recognized Tribal government with jurisdiction over the area in which the proposed environmental justice project is located; or

(C) a Tribal organization that demonstrates that it has worked directly with the affected community, as determined by the Administrator.

(3) ENVIRONMENTAL JUSTICE PROJECT.—The term "environmental justice project" means a project consisting of activities designed to empower and educate an affected community to—

(A) understand environmental and public health issues; and

(B) identify ways to address those issues at the local level.

(d) AUTHORIZATION OF APPROPRIATIONS.—There is authorized to be appropriated to carry out this section $16,000,000 for each fiscal year.

House Committee on the Judiciary Bill 7

Title: H.R. 83 Mobilizing Against Sanctuary Cities Act

Sponsor: Representative Lou Barletta [PA-11] (introduced 01/03/2017)

Summary: This bill prohibits a state or local government from receiving federal financial assistance for a minimum of one year if it restricts or prohibits a government entity or official from: (1) sending to or receiving from the responsible federal immigration agency information regarding an individual's citizenship or immigration status, or (2) maintaining or exchanging information about an individual's status.

The bill restores assistance eligibility upon a Department of Justice (DOJ) determination that the jurisdiction no longer restricts or prohibits such actions.

DOJ shall report each year to Congress regarding state or local jurisdictions that restrict or prohibit such actions.

FULL TEXT:

A BILL

To prohibit the receipt of Federal financial assistance by sanctuary cities, and for other purposes.

Be it enacted by the Senate and House of Representatives of the United States of America in Congress assembled,

SECTION 1. SHORT TITLE.

This Act may be cited as the "Mobilizing Against Sanctuary Cities Act".

SEC. 2. SANCTUARY CITIES INELIGIBLE FOR FEDERAL FINANCIAL ASSISTANCE.

Any State or local government that violates section 642 of the Illegal Immigration Reform and Immigrant Responsibility Act of 1996 may not receive any Federal financial assistance (as such term is defined in section 7501(a)(5) of title 31, United States Code). The Attorney General shall determine annually which State or local jurisdictions are not in compliance with section 642 of the Illegal Immigration Reform and Immigrant Responsibility Act and shall report such determinations to Congress on March 1 of each year. The Attorney General shall also issue a report concerning the compliance of any particular State or local jurisdiction at the request of any Member of Congress. Any jurisdiction that is found to be out of compliance shall be ineligible to receive Federal financial assistance for a minimum period of one year, and shall only become eligible again after the Attorney General certifies that the jurisdiction is in compliance.

House Committee on the Judiciary Bill 8

Title: 8. H.R. 2437 Back the Blue Act of 2017

Sponsor: Representative Ted Poe [TX-2] (Introduced 5/16/2017)

Summary: This bill amends the federal criminal code by establishing mandatory minimum sentences of 10 years in prison for offenders who kill, or attempt or conspire to kill, current or former U.S. judges and federal law enforcement officers. Offenders are subject to 30 years in prison or the death penalty if death results.

FULL TEXT:

A BILL

To protect law enforcement officers, and for other purposes.

Be it enacted by the Senate and House of Representatives of the United States of America in Congress assembled,

SECTION 1. SHORT TITLE.

This Act may be cited as the "Back the Blue Act of 2017".

SEC. 2. PROTECTION OF LAW ENFORCEMENT OFFICERS.

(a) KILLING OF LAW ENFORCEMENT OFFICERS.—

    (1) OFFENSE.—Chapter 51 of title 18, United States Code, is amended by adding at the end the following:

"§ 1123. Killing of law enforcement officers

    "(b) OFFENSE.—It shall be unlawful for any person to—

        "(1) kill, or attempt or conspire to kill—

            "(A) a United States judge;

            "(B) a Federal law enforcement officer; or

            "(C) a federally funded public safety officer while that officer is engaged in official duties, or on account of the performance of official duties; or

        "(2) kill a former United States judge, Federal law enforcement officer, or federally funded public safety officer on account of the past performance of official duties.

    "(c) PENALTY.—Any person that violates subsection (b) shall be fined under this title and imprisoned for not less than 10 years or for life, or, if death results, shall be sentenced to not less than 30 years and not more than life, or may be punished by death.".

(b) ASSAULT OF LAW ENFORCEMENT OFFICERS.—

    (1) OFFENSE.—Chapter 7 of title 18, United States Code, is amended by adding at the end the following:

"§ 120. Assaults of law enforcement officers

    "(b) OFFENSE.—It shall be unlawful to assault a federally funded State or local law enforcement officer while engaged in or on account of the performance of official duties, or assaults any person who formerly served as a federally funded State or local law enforcement officer on account of the performance of such person's official duties during such service, or because of the actual or perceived status of the person as a federally funded State or local law enforcement officer.

    "(c) PENALTY.—Any person that violates subsection (b) shall be subject to a fine under this title and—

        "(1) if the assault resulted in bodily injury (as defined in section 1365), shall be imprisoned not less than 2 years and not more than 10 years;

        "(2) if the assault resulted in substantial bodily injury (as defined in section 113), shall be imprisoned not less than 5 years and not more than 20 years;

        "(3) if the assault resulted in serious bodily injury (as defined in section 1365), shall be imprisoned for not less than 10 years;

        "(4) if a deadly or dangerous weapon was used during and in relation to the assault, shall be imprisoned for not less than 20 years; and

        "(5) shall be imprisoned for not more than 1 year in any other case.

Committee of the Whole Debating Rules

FLOOR DEBATE

1. The **Speaker will call the House to order** and open Legislative Business of the day.[1]
2. All members are expected to have read all bills under consideration. Therefore, **bills will be introduced by their titles only** and not read in their entirety.
3. The Speaker will remind the members of the rules attached to each bill as it is introduced. **Each party will have the same amount of total time to make speeches on each bill.** The majority will get the opening speech, after which the order will rotate back and forth across the aisle.
4. Typically, the majority party (more, specifically, the chairman of the committee with jurisdiction over the bill) chairs the debate. In this simulation the instructor (or designee) will manage the time and the **Speaker will act as the chair,** recognizing representatives from both parties.
5. The rules attached to each bill dictate the **maximum amount of time each representative may speak, somewhere between 30 and 90 seconds.** If a member does not use his or her full allotment, he or she yields the balance of their time back to their party. If a member needs additional time to speak, he or she must request more time from the Speaker.
6. **If another member would like to ask a question of the person speaking, he or she should address the Speaker** and ask "Will the gentleman from Massachusetts yield to me?" If the gentleman/woman agrees, he or she will spend his or her allotted time responding to the question at his/her discretion.

---

[1] In Congress, a number of precursory steps would occur first, such as a prayer, approval of the House Journal, the Pledge of Allegiance, etc.

AMENDMENTS

A representative may, upon being recognized by the Speaker AND if the rules allow it—choose to offer an amendment instead of a speech. The amendment must be relevant to the bill (or what is known as "germane"), and must be straightforward so that others are clear on the change that is being proposed. The instructor may choose to write the amendment up on the board. The representative who offers the amendment will have 2 minutes to speak in favor of it. Any one representative who is opposed to the amendment (of either party) may have up to 2 minutes to respond. This will not be subtracted from allotted time for either party.

Next, the Speaker will ask those in favor of adopted the amendment to say "aye" and those opposed to say "no." The instructor (or designee) will count the votes and announce the outcome.

If time for debate remains on the bill under consideration, debate will resume—either on the bill in its amended form (if the amendment passes) or in its original form (if the amendment fails). Multiple amendments may be introduced and considered on any bill that allows them.

CODE OF CONDUCT

The following rules are taken *directly* from the House of Representatives[2]—and will be applicable to our simulation with the exception of the dress code, which is optional.

A Member should avoid impugning the motives of another Member, the Senate, the Vice President or the President, using offensive language, or uttering words that are otherwise deemed unparliamentary.

Relevancy: A Member may get carried away in debate and stray from the subject under discussion.

Addressing the Chair: A Member must be standing while speaking.

Dress Code: Members should dress appropriately which has traditionally been considered to include a coat and tie for male Members and appropriate attire for female Members. Members should not wear overcoats or hats on the Floor while the House is in session.

There is no eating, drinking, or smoking permitted. The use of personal electronic equipment, including cellular telephones and laptop computers, is banned on the Floor of the House.

Forms of Address: Members should not address their colleagues by name on the House Floor. They are "the Gentleman from California," or "the Gentleman from California, Mr. Jones" or "the Gentlewoman from Florida," or "the Gentlewoman from Florida, Mrs. Smith."

---

[2] http://democrats.rules.house.gov/archives/floor_man.htm#X

SAMPLE DIALOGUE

Speaker: "We will now consider Bill 4. There are no amendments allowed on this bill and each party will have 5 minutes total. Representative can speak for no more than 45 seconds. Who would like to be recognized? [Representatives raise their hands and the Speaker selects a representative from the majority party first.] "I recognize the Gentleman from California."

Representative from California: "Hello colleagues, I am against this bill because ..."

Instructor: "Time."

Representative from California: "Mr. Speaker, I ask unanimous consent to revise and extend my remarks."

Speaker: "One additional minute is granted to the Gentleman from California."

Representative from Texas: "Mr. Speaker (or Madam Speaker), will the gentleman from California yield to me?"

Speaker: "Your answer, Gentleman from California?"

Representative from California: "Yes" (or "No").

Representative from Texas: "I'm wondering if the Gentleman from California can explain why ..."

Representative from California: "The reason is ..."

Instructor: "Time."

Speaker: "I recognize the Gentlewoman from Ohio."

Representative from Ohio: "I am in favor of this bill because ... I yield the balance of my time to the Speaker."

Appendix

Appendix

Representative Worksheet

Background Information

I. Learn about your district.
1. Find a map of the district and a map of the state. Where is the district located in the state? (Hint: There will be a link to a map of the district from the representative's Web site.)

_____

2. Learn at least three things about the people who live there. For example, what types of jobs/industry are there? How diverse is the district? What is the annual income of people who live there? What is the average education level? Is it urban or rural? (Hint: You can search for this information by looking at U.S. Census data, visiting the state's Web site, or searching for the district itself, i.e., "California 7th Congressional District.")

a)_____

b)_____

c)_____

II. Learn about your representative.
1. How long has your representative been in Congress?

_____

2. What did your representative do before being elected to Congress?

_____

_____

_____

3. Is your representative married? Does he or she have children?

_____

4. What issues does your representative care deeply about?

_____

_____

III. Go to the committee Web site for the committee that you will be working in for Mock Congress. In the real House of Representatives, your representative serves on more than one committee, but for this simulation you will only serve on one committee. (See the list of participants to find out which one you are on.)
Find the following information. (Hint: You can search online for the committee by title, i.e., "House Ways and Means Committee.")

1. Who is the current chairperson of the committee?

_____

2. How many Democrats and how many Republicans currently serve on this committee? (Hint: There will be a list of all committee members on the Web site; the majority party will always have more people than the minority party.)

_____

IV. Visit at least one of the following Web sites to investigate campaign donations. Put in the name of your representative and see what you find out about individuals, companies, or organizations that have donated money to your representative in their recent election campaigns:
http://www.fec.gov/DisclosureSearch/mapApp.do
http://www.followthemoney.org/
http://www.opensecrets.org

_____

_____

_____

_____

V. Can you find a video of an interview, speech, or debate by your representative? What is it about? What does your representative say?

_____

_____

_____

_____

Preparation for Committee Work

VI. Read both of the bills your committee will be working on. Briefly summarize what each proposes to do.

1. _____

_____

_____

_____

2. _____

_____

_____

_____

VII. Develop three questions regarding each bill that will help you formulate an opinion.

1.

a) _____

_____

_____

b) _____

_____

_____

c) _____

_____

_____

2.

a) _____

_____

_____

b) _____

_____

_____

c) _____

_____

_____

VIII. Decide whether you think your representative would lean toward voting for or voting against the bills under consideration in your committee, and explain why. (Note: You can change your mind at any time!)

1. _____

_____

_____

2. _____

_____

_____

Leader Worksheet

Background Information

I. Learn about your district.

    1. Find a map of the district and a map of the state. Where is the district located in the state? (Hint: There will be a link to a map of the district from the representative's Web site.)

    _____

    2. Learn at least three things about the people who live there. For example, what types of jobs/industry are there? How diverse is the district? What is the annual income of people who live there? What is the average education level? Is it urban or rural? (Hint: You can search for this information by looking at U.S. Census data, visiting the state's Web site, or searching for the district itself, i.e., "California 7th Congressional District.")

    a)_____

    b)_____

    c)_____

II. Learn about your representative.

   1. How long has your representative been in Congress?

   _____

   2. What did your representative do before he or she was in Congress?

   _____

   _____

   _____

   3. Is your representative married? Does your representative have children?

   _____

   4. What issues does your representative seem to care deeply about?

   _____

   _____

III. Go to the Web site of your leadership position. What is different about this page from your district page?

   _____

   _____

   _____

   What is the current breakdown (in numbers) between Democrats and Republicans in the House of Representatives?

   _____

   IV. Look over the list of participants. Try to introduce yourself to at least five members of your party prior to committee work.

V. Can you find a video of an interview, speech, or debate by your representative? What is it about? What does your representative say?

_____

_____

_____

_____

PREPARATION FOR COMMITTEE WORK

VI. Read the bills each committee will be working on. Briefly summarize what each bill is about, and consider: a) how you would vote as a representative for your district; b) how you would advise your party members to vote as a caucus.

1._____
_____
_____
_____
_____

2._____
_____
_____
_____
_____

3._____
_____
_____
_____
_____

4._____
_____
_____
_____
_____

5._____
_____
_____
_____
_____

6._____
_____
_____
_____
_____

7._____
_____
_____
_____
_____

8._____
_____
_____
_____
_____

VII. Meet with the other leaders of your party, and make sure you are all on the same page. You may want to exchange contact information in order to strategize in advance of committee work.

Lobbyist Worksheet

To prepare, you must research your employer, study the bills, and prepare talking points for the positions you plan to take.

Background Information

I. Learn about your employer.

   1. Summarize their mission statement (or equivalent explanation of purpose):

_____

_____

_____

_____

   2. How large is this organization? Can you find out how much money they spend on lobbying?

_____

_____

_____

_____

   3. What kinds of policies do they advocate in favor of?

a)_____

b)_____

c)_____

4. What kinds of policies do they advocate against?

a)_____

b)_____

c)_____

Preparation for Committee Work

II. Read the bills you will be working on. Briefly summarize what each bill is about.

1._____
_____
_____
_____

2._____
_____
_____
_____

3._____
_____
_____
_____

III. Do you think that one political party or representatives from certain areas or backgrounds will be particularly amenable—or opposed—to your point of view? Explain.

_____
_____
_____
_____
_____
_____
_____

IV. Develop five talking points for each bill that you could use to sway representatives to your way of thinking.

Bill #_____

1._____
2._____
3._____
4._____
5._____

Bill #_____

1._____
2._____
3._____
4._____
5._____

Bill #_____

1._____
2._____
3._____
4._____
5._____

Witness Worksheet

To prepare, you must study the bills. Get ready to respond to questions posed by the committee members.

PREPARATION FOR COMMITTEE WORK

I. Read the bills you will be working on. Briefly summarize what each bill is about.

Bill #_____

_____

_____

_____

_____

_____

Bill #_____

_____

_____

_____

_____

_____

II. Brainstorm a list of potential questions that representatives might ask you.

Role 1: _____

_____

_____

_____

_____

_____

Role 2: _____

_____

_____

_____

_____

_____

III. Search online and take notes on information that will help prepare you to give testimony. Below are some organizations, news media, and other resources. Of course, you are encouraged to go beyond these resources! Ask your instructor if you need help finding information, or are unsure about any aspect of the roles you will take on. Witnesses who are testifying on the same bills might also benefit from working together (Witnesses A and B, Witnesses C and D).

Witness A
Role 1—Senior Education Policy Specialist with the National Conference of State Legislatures

National Conference on State Legislatures: School Vouchers
http://www.ncsl.org/research/education/school-choice-vouchers.aspx

Education Commission of the States
http://www.ecs.org/50-state-comparison-vouchers/

Education Choice
https://www.edchoice.org/

Witness A
Role 2—Director of the U.S. Fish and Wildlife Agency

U.S. Fish and Wildlife Agency
https://www.fws.gov/

Greenpeace
http://www.greenpeace.org/usa/

Oceana
http://usa.oceana.org/

Witness B
Role 1—Oil and gas well drilling expert

American Petroleum Institute
http://www.api.org/oil-and-natural-gas

U.S. Energy Information & Analysis
http://www/eia.gov/energyexplained/index.cfm

Natural Gas
http://www.naturalgas.org/

Witness B
Role 2—Co-Chair of the National Coalition for Public Education

National Coalition for Public Education
https://www.ncpecoalition.org/vouchers/

Center for Public Education
http://www.centerforpubliceducation.org/

Americans United
https://www.au.org/issues/school-vouchers-government-subsidies-religious-schools

Witness C
Role 1—Executive Director of the Electronic Privacy Information Center

Electronic Privacy Information Center
https://www.epic.org/
https://www.epic.org/privacy/drones/

Federal Aviation Administration
https://www.faa.gov/uas/

Witness C
Role 2—Executive Director of the United States Conference of Mayors.

U.S. Conference of Mayors
https://www.usmayors.org/

Center for American Progress (Articles on Sanctuary Cities)
https://www.americanprogress.org/issues/immigration/
reports/2017/01/26/297366/the-effects-of-sanctuary-policies-on-crime-
and-the-economy/

https://www.americanprogress.org/issues/immigration/news/2017/03/07/427438/
how-much-funding-for-sanctuary-jurisdictions-could-be-at-risk/

The Sentencing Project
http://www.sentencingproject.org/publications/immigration-public-safety/

Witness D
Role 1—Acting Director of U.S. Immigration and Customs Enforcement

U.S. Immigration and Customs Enforcement
https://www.ice.gov/
https://www.ice.gov/declined-detainer-outcome-report

The Heritage Foundation
http://www.heritage.org/immigration

Witness D
Role 2—Research Fellow at the Brookings Institute's Center for Technology Innovation

Brookings Institute's Center for Technology Innovation
https://www.brookings.edu/center/center-for-technology-innovation/

Article on Drones and Privacy
http://www.chicagotribune.com/news/opinion/commentary/ct-drones-privacy-
laws-20150803-story.html

IV. Develop five talking points for each role that appropriately represents your point of view.

Role 1: _____

1. _____

2. _____

3. _____

4. _____

5. _____

Role 2: _____

1. _____

2. _____

3. _____

4. _____

5. _____

Rules Sheet

Rules Sheet Recommendation for Bill #_____
Submit this sheet for each bill that passes out of committee.

1. How long will <u>each party</u> have in total to speak in support of or against this bill? Circle one:

3 Minutes   4 Minutes   5 Minutes   6 Minutes

2. What is the maximum amount of time an individual representative will be allowed to speak during a single speech for or against this bill? Circle one:

30 Seconds   45 Seconds   60 Seconds   90 Seconds

3. Will amendments be allowed? Circle one:

Open rule (amendments)   Closed rule (no amendments)

Has the bill been altered? If so, please note ALL changes here and/or attach the marked up bill(s).